Psychic Development

Psychic Development for Beginners, Teaching you to Unlock your Psychic Abilities and Open your Third Eye!

Table of Contents

Introduction 1

Chapter 1 – What are Psychic Abilities? 2

Chapter 2 – Reasons to Develop your Psychic Abilities 7

Chapter 3 – How to Develop your Psychic Abilities 10

Chapter 4 – Viewing Auras 15

Chapter 5 – The Third Eye 25

Chapter 6 – How to Strengthen your Intuition 34

Chapter 7 – Spirit Guides and How You can Connect with Them
.... 41

Chapter 8 – Mistakes to Avoid When Developing your Psychic
Abilities 48

Conclusion 51

Introduction

Thank you for taking the time to read this book on psychic development!

This book covers the topic of psychic development and will teach you how to improve your psychic abilities. If you have ever thought that you may have some psychic abilities lying dormant, then this book is for you! With the help of this book you will be able to recognize your own psychic abilities, and then develop them with proven strategies in a safe and effective manner.

In the following chapters, you will discover what the different psychic abilities are, and how each one can be developed specifically. You will learn about interpreting your dreams, developing your intuition, viewing auras, and connecting with spirit guides, along with much more!

At the completion of this book, you will have a good understanding of how to improve your psychic abilities and will be well on your way to becoming a powerful and consciously aware psychic!

Once again, thanks for choosing this book, I hope you find it to be helpful!

Chapter 1 – What are Psychic Abilities?

Have you ever had a strange premonition about something that turned out to be true? Maybe you had a strong feeling that your friend was in trouble. Perhaps you correctly predicted that something bad was about to happen. Or it could simply be the time when you predicted that your phone would ring, and that a particular person would be calling.

If these kinds of instances have occurred more than once, then there is a great chance that you have psychic ability; the ability to perceive details concealed from a person's normal senses through ESP (extrasensory perception). While having this ability is a bit strange, scary, and overwhelming at first, it is actually quite a gift.

Some psychics believe that they have a few spiritual or intuitive abilities. Others, on the other hand, recognize only a single psychic skill. If you are still trying to figure out whether you have psychic abilities, then check out the following signs of being a psychic and determine how many of them are true in your case:

- **High levels of intuition** – Some situations that display this ability include knowing who is calling you before you even pick up your phone, and predicting an event before it actually happens.

- **Experiencing déjà vu often** – You may have felt like you have been in a certain place before, despite having never actually been there. Déjà vu could also be characterized by a strong familiarity with things, places, events, and people. You may feel like you are re-living certain moments and feel a strong sense of familiarity that cannot be explained by logic. If you experience these things, then it is possible that you have a psychic ability.

- **Spirit dreams** – The departed often visit their loved ones when they are asleep. It is because this is the time when the vulnerability and openness of your subconscious mind are at their peak. However, unlike most people, psychics tend to receive more regular visits not only from their departed loved ones but also from other people they don't know in their dreams.

- **Always accurate gut feeling** – Your instinct may be so strong that you know something before it actually happens. You can sense current or future events, which strongly indicates that you are a psychic.

- **Telepathic instances** – These instances include sending messages using your mind, reading the thought process of those around you, and developing a mind-to-mind connection. Experiencing these things from time to time signifies that you have one of the most common forms of psychic ability, which is telepathy.

- **You can sense trouble** – You may have that feeling that someone close to you will be in trouble. It can cause fear and discomfort, especially if you can't find any reason for why you seem to sense danger.

Other possible signs that you are a psychic include feeling overwhelmed when exposed to public spaces, visualizing things, places, or people that you have not seen before, having the ability to finish others' sentences, and feeling the pain of others and the energy in a building or house. Your psychic power is also imminent if you have vivid imaginations and inner dialogues, hear voices or sounds that other people can't hear, and have the ability to heal, and tell or predict the future.

If you experience at least one of the signs mentioned, then it confirms the presence of your psychic power. It's quite common to feel afraid once you first realize that you have this skill, but remember, developing it is actually a gift. The wise use of this gift can make your life even better.

If you are still on the verge of developing your psychic abilities, then understanding its various types can help. By understanding each psychic ability, you can figure out which ones you'd like to develop further.

Astral Projection

Through astral projection, you can put yourself into several scenarios, including near-death experiences and lucid dreams. One popular application of astral projection is separating your soul from your physical body.

While this specific kind of psychic experience works similarly to out of body experiences (OBE), it is still important to take note of their differences. One is the fact that OBE is involuntary, while astral projection is voluntary. In most cases, you can achieve this experience through proper meditation. It lets your soul or astral body travel to certain places that your physical body can't (ex. through doors and walls).

Channeling/Mediumship

Channeling or mediumship refers to a psychic ability, which lets you directly communicate with spirits. It turns you into a medium who is capable of talking to those who have passed away. You can convey the messages of spirits to their intended living recipients; usually the loved ones of the departed.

While mediumship comes in various forms, the most common form is the ability to hear and speak to spirits, and then convey the message to the intended recipient. A less common form is where the spirit partially takes over the medium's body and is able to speak directly through them. This could be through verbal speech, or through writing or drawing.

Aura Reading

Aura reading is another psychic ability that you should be aware of. With this skill, you can perceive the energy fields that surround not only people, but also things and places. Psychics believe that all living things have an aura, which represents a magnetic energy field. What these psychics can do is sense, see, and feel the aura surrounding a physical body.

While such energy fields are not visible to most people, gifted psychics can see them clearly. In fact, having this ability will let you read an aura, giving you a clearer idea about what other people are feeling (whether they are happy, sad, sick, or healthy). It also lets you read any disruption in a person's aura, making it possible for you to send a timely warning.

Reading the aura, which surrounds an animal, object, or person is a common psychic ability. Psychics can see various colors in the aura and ascribe various meanings to each one. Someone who can read auras can also see the colorful variations of these energy fields. With that, they can provide insights about the spiritual, physical, mental, and emotional nature of the person they were able to read.

Intuition

You have a high level of intuition if you find it easy to feel a clear and intimate knowledge of things. Having this psychic ability means that you can grab insights that are no longer part of the normal thought process. Note that in psychic development, intuition plays a major part. In fact, it contributes a lot in honing various psychic skills.

Many describe it as the innate sense of feelings, thoughts, events, and activities of others that the normal human capacity can no longer perceive. For instance, a person who has an extraordinary intuition may instantly sense that someone is an alcoholic, even if this problem is not visible based on the way he looks and carries himself.

Someone who has this ability also possesses a borderline perception. It is a vital part of your sixth sense, giving you the gift to know or be aware of the things that do not come from logic or observation. Since it is the sixth sense, it is safe to say that everyone possesses this ability to some extent.

However, there are those who excel in it. It frequently comes in the form of a gut feeling, which will serve as your internal guide.

Telepathy

This psychic ability makes it possible for you to communicate with someone without physically interacting with him. Telepathy lets you send info from one person to another, without any physical interaction or obvious communication.

Telepathy comes in different forms – one of which is telepathic impression. It involves planting an image, word, or message into another person's mind. There is also what we call mind reading. This lets you sense the thoughts that are in the minds of others.

Another form of telepathy is mind control. This lets you partially control someone's thoughts and actions by giving them commands. This psychic power promotes mind-to-mind communication, giving the psychic the chance to communicate complete and clear thoughts in the blink of an eye.

Note that telepathy does not only work on humans. Animal telepathy is also another of its popular forms, which gives the psychic the power to communicate with animals.

Empathy

Psychics who have empathic skills can feel the emotions and physical pains of another person. While this skill is involuntary, remind yourself that once you develop it, you can still learn to control the way you react to the confusing feelings and emotions that do not belong to you.

Empathy is a skill that most people have, although in different degrees. Those who are able to hone it can sense one's emotions without physical cues. What they do is detect the energy that a person is putting out.

Chapter 2 – Reasons to Develop your Psychic Abilities

Now that you know some of the most common psychic abilities, it is time to learn the specific reasons why you should develop these skills. The following benefits of psychic development will most likely serve as your motivation to turn yourself into a more proficient psychic:

It raises your awareness of what is happening around you.

For instance, you can instantly sense if a loved one is sad. You can sense their feelings right away, even if they try to hide it. You may also find this useful in your career. For instance, you can spot those who are fooling you during negotiations.

Your extrasensory perception will be able to provide you with plenty of vital information that can improve your awareness of the world surrounding you; particularly events and people. This can give you a strong strategic advantage in all areas of your life.

It promotes self-improvement.

Psychic development will also help you to improve yourself. This is because you can learn new things from doing it. It helps you improve your mind, mental and physical skills, memory, and efficiency. Developing your psychic abilities can also lead you to develop a lot of interesting skills. An example would be developing better focus through meditation.

It expands your consciousness.

By developing your psychic abilities, your consciousness will also improve. You may only be a simple person with a regular 9 to 5 job, but after you develop your skills, you will start feeling extraordinary. You will feel that way once you start using your ability to your advantage. For instance, you could start seeing the auras of people surrounding you, allowing you to delve deeper into their feelings and thoughts.

This is a big help in expanding your consciousness. It lets you develop your understanding of how things work, which can also help you build good traits, such as being kind and helpful to others. Your expanded consciousness can also lead you to the path of spiritual growth. Just imagine where certain skills, like astral projection and psychic empathy, could take you.

It opens up several business opportunities.

Developing your psychic skill opens up several business opportunities. For one, you can build a professional psychic business using your ability. This will let you provide psychic readings and advice, perform psychic healing, and remove the negative energies of certain places, among other professional services that you can offer. You can earn money while giving yourself the chance to help those who need your service.

It gives you a greater pulling power.

Having psychic powers promotes a blessed and full life. Psychic abilities allow you to feel a sense of intuition, which can be a great guiding force in your life. You can make big decisions even during unusual circumstances with such guidance.

It brings reassurance and comfort.

Psychic development can also bring you reassurance and comfort. This is a big advantage for you, especially if you have had traumatic experiences in the past. It can give you peace of mind, knowing that there is a greater force that is with you.

There are indeed several reasons why you should continue developing your psychic powers. Aside from the reasons and benefits already mentioned, deciding to hone your psychic skills will let you tap into certain abilities that are already within yourself.

In addition, psychic development can help improve your confidence. It can improve your focus and mental clarity and give you a new purpose in life. You can also use this process to discover more about your potential talents, and use your developed psychic power to attain success and prosperity.

Chapter 3 – How to Develop your Psychic Abilities

Professional psychics are capable of tapping into one's subconscious mind. While most people have psychic skills, too much clutter can cloud them. There are also those who are fully aware that they have psychic powers but are unsure how to use and enhance them.

It's important to note that you can fine-tune, bring out, and hone your psychic abilities using the right methods. While in most cases you need to use methods that are specific to the kind of ability you wish to hone, there are still general steps and tips that you can follow. Here are some strategies for improving your psychic abilities:

Meditate for around 10 to 15 minutes every day

If you want to develop your psychic abilities, then you need to raise your vibration. This is important because spirit energy tends to vibrate at a higher level and frequency. In this pursuit, meditation can definitely help. It does so by putting you in a more relaxed state, thus raising your vibration. Meditating every day lets you connect more to your higher self and spirit, as well as to the energy of other people.

Develop your psychic hearing

Also called clairaudience, psychic hearing plays a major role in transforming yourself into a real psychic. What you have to do to develop it is to lay quietly and peacefully in bed right before sleeping. Spend a few minutes listening to all the sounds surrounding you. Your focus should be on the sounds that you usually ignore. It could be the sound of crickets, or of the wind. By focusing on these sounds, you can sharpen your intuitive gift, which is essential when trying to develop your psychic powers.

Practice journaling often

What is good about journaling is that it lets you connect with your soul or higher self and your spiritual helpers. To perform this correctly, think of a certain scenario that may require you to seek guidance. Journal about the mentioned scenario. When doing this, ensure that you let yourself relax so you can start receiving divine guidance.

Keeping a dream journal can also help. Note that right from the start of honing your psychic skills, it's common to begin having vivid dreams. If you have such dreams, then having a dream journal around can help you to remember and interpret them.

Improve your psychic ability through small objects

You can also use small objects, those that you can easily find at home when honing your psychic powers. Some psychics, particularly those who are dealing with criminal investigations, make use of clothing. The main goal here is to look for an object that has already been used as this is guaranteed to have higher energy when compared to an unused one.

Once you have chosen an object, put it in your hands. With your eyes closed, relax, and then feel the object and focus on what your body feels. You may start asking yourself important questions, like the gender of the owner of the object, his/her past career, and any emotions attached to the object or person.

Anything that comes to your mind, especially in the form of a gut feeling or instinct should then be written down. This process is known as the energetic impression. Once you receive the information you need, avoid editing anything so you can compare the things you have written down with the actual facts.

Hone your skill to feel empathy

A real and professional psychic is someone who is acutely in tune with the emotions, energy, and pain of others. In fact, it is possible for many psychics to experience the things experienced by others as if it were happening to them personally. Therefore, if you want to develop your psychic powers, you have to learn a thing or two about cultivating empathy.

One method is to be an expert when it comes to reading body language. Note that most psychics learn several things about a certain person through their ability to read and understand non-verbal cues. Such can offer key predictors showing one's inner feelings.

You can also perceive the emotions of others better by putting your hands on them.

Develop your concentration

You need to develop your concentration if you want to be a psychic. Your full concentration is vital if you wish to perceive the inner thoughts of other people or use your mind to move objects. One exercise for developing your concentration involves holding a picture for a few minutes while looking closely at it.

Close your eyes and then reproduce the picture with all the details you can remember using your mind. This is a visualization technique that can help boost your concentration. Use the power of daydreaming and imagination, too. This will let you activate your subconscious, which is actually a big help in boosting your psychic power.

Free yourself from any negative energy

To raise your sensitivity to the experiences and emotions of those around you, focus on using your own energy at a higher level or frequency. Work on removing negativity from your life first, though. Note that negativity can cloud your psychic power, so you have to get rid of it as much as possible. Start filling your mind and aura with positivity.

Be quiet and still

Note that quietness and stillness can give you the kind of peace you need to bring in natural energy. What you have to do to be quiet and still is to spend some time every day away from the clutter of modern life. Free yourself from all forms of distraction so you can perceive positive energy better.

Freeing yourself from noisy distractions allows you to think more clearly, which is helpful in improving your focus and inner mental accuracy. Spend some time basking into the beauty of nature. The natural echoes of your surroundings can also boost your psychic abilities and intuition. Ensure that you are away from electronic devices that might distract you. This includes your TV, cellphone, and laptop, among many others.

Have faith in yourself

Your negative thoughts can block your psychic powers, so avoid succumbing to them as much as possible. You may feel disappointed during the early stages of developing your psychic powers, especially if you are unable to get the results you want. But you should avoid letting this negativity affect you. No matter how long it takes to develop the skill, continue believing in yourself and staying upbeat.

Make it a point to look for inspiration wherever and whenever possible. Start reading the stories of those who were able to hone their psychic skills and find ways to follow in their footsteps. Release any doubts from your mind. Let yourself trust your natural power and supernatural powers. Always give your 100 percent effort. Do not leave any room for doubt and skepticism during your spiritual endeavors.

Overcome your fears

Psychic contact, as well as other supernatural phenomena, can be terrifying at first. However, you should avoid letting fear get into you as it can block your ability. If you wish to be in touch with your spirituality, you should overcome your fear of its consequences. Note that while developing your psychic powers, you may start foreseeing new things that you did not expect.

Remember that this will always be a part of your experience so ensure that you embrace this gift. Every time your fear gets in the way of your psychic development, fill your mind with all the good things that this power can do for you.

Expand your imagination

You need to expand your imagination if you wish to improve your remote viewing ability. Remote viewing refers to the psychic skill of visiting places using your mind. This means that there is no need for you to visit the place physically. Practice by visualizing every place you wish to visit the next day. Imagine anything – from the department or grocery store to your friend's house.

Imagine that you are in that place before sleeping. Take note of the colors, objects, and people you visualized in your dream. After that, identify the ones that match prior to going there personally and looking around. Writing down your dreams with an aim of letting them stay fresh in your mind can help in expanding your imagination.

Practice

Continue practicing even if your results are slow at first. Keep in mind that it takes time and effort to gain your desired psychic power, so make it a point to practice every day.

Honing your abilities to perfection may even take years, but you have to trust in the process. Believe that your skills will surface and improve sooner or later, and do not lose hope.

Chapter 4 – Viewing Auras

Aura reading is one of the most common psychic powers that you can develop. Learning how to view and read the aura of other people is a major help in your psychic development journey. Auras actually refer to the energy fields that all humans emit. These auras differ not only in color, but also in intensity. Some psychics see auras as a glow of light surrounding someone. By sensing and reading auras, you can improve your ability to perceive the thoughts of those surrounding you.

When it comes to improving your ability to view auras, a complete understanding of their different layers is a must. Also referred to as subtle bodies, these aura layers can supply you with relevant information. Each layer corresponds to a certain chakra, which also creates energies that produce the aura that you need to view. Also, take note that certain factors affect how big or small the aura is. These factors include your spiritual, physical, and emotional health. You can expect the auric layers to expand and contract based on these factors.

Here are the different layers of aura that you should take note of:

Etheric Layer

This is the first known layer of the aura. It is around one-half to two inches in size from the skin's surface, outlining your body. This energy field primarily connects with the first chakra as well as your meridians, glands, and body organs. It has a strong relationship with the present health and condition of your physical body.

The etheric layer is known to be the closest to your physical body. Aside from representing your body, it also characterizes your bones, tissues, and muscles. It tends to pulsate at twenty cycles every minute. You can also expect this layer to be stronger in active people, especially athletes. It tends to be weaker in those who have a weak immunity and follow a sedentary lifestyle.

Emotional Layer

The emotional layer is the second layer of your aura, which extends 2-4 inches from your physical body. It encircles your body in an oval shape. It is connected to your second chakra, as well as your experiences and emotions. This layer reflects your current mood and stores some of your unsettled emotions, like loneliness, resentment, and fear.

The energies that form part of the emotional layer will connect to the first layer. It then processes the information into your physical body. Bombarding the first layer with the emotional pain that resides in this second layer of aura can result in muscle cramps, upset stomach, and physical tension. You can use your familiarity with the emotional layer to determine the state of one's chakras.

Mental Layer

As the third layer of aura, the mental layer is connected to your third chakra, as well as your logical processes, intellect, ideas, consciousness, and belief systems. It can extend from 4 to 8 inches from your physical body. This is the specific layer where you can rationalize and validate your ideas and thoughts. This is also where mental issues and mental health can present themselves.

The mental layer is higher and finer in vibration when compared to the emotional layer. It tends to radiate strongly around your neck, shoulders, and head. This aura layer also tends to be strong in people who are often involved in mental tasks as well as those with overactive minds.

Astral Layer

The fourth layer is called the astral layer, which is linked to the areas of expression of your mental, emotional, and ethereal layers. It is also linked to your heart chakra, which is known as the chakra of love and balance. Note that while the first three mentioned aura layers reflect your physical presence and nature, the astral layer serves as the window to your spiritual nature. This makes this specific layer distinguishable from the other three.

It is possible to strengthen this layer through intimate and loving relationships. It tends to get weaker when you are in conflict with your loved ones and during breakups. Just like the third layer, you can also use the astral layer to see the state of one's chakras.

Etheric Template Layer

The next layer is referred to as the etheric template. It is connected to your fifth chakra, as well as to your creativity, vibration, sound, and communication. You can find a blueprint containing all forms of the physical world within this field. This aura layer also serves as a blueprint of your physical body within the spiritual plane.

The etheric template encompasses all the things that you create on a physical level. These include your overall personality, energy, and identity. You can heal and strengthen this layer through your full awareness of your true self and the expression of your truth.

Celestial Layer

The celestial layer is the next aura layer that you have to familiarize yourself with. It is the specific layer where your physical mind connects with the spiritual mind using devotional practices and meditation. Aside from being linked to the 6th chakra, it is also connected to dreams, trust, unconditional love, honesty, spiritual awareness, memories, and intuitive knowledge.

This layer also possesses your experiences of connecting to something, which is bigger and greater than yourself. You can also associate it with enlightenment. It is composed of light, which lets you access a higher intellectual knowledge, information, and wisdom that are present in your collective consciousness. Once you strengthen this, you can hone the power to receive angelic messages and communicate with the spiritual world.

Ketheric Template

This is the last aura layer that an aspiring psychic should be aware of. What this layer holds are all the details and info related to your previous lifetimes as well as your soul. It also symbolizes the feeling of oneness with the universe. It is linked to the universal and divine consciousness.

The ketheric template layer also contains your soul contract or life plan. It is reflective of all the experiences and expertise passed on by the soul during the present life. Strengthening the ketheric template improves your ability to surrender to the Divine path, which is helpful when it comes to enhancing your psychic skills.

How to View Auras?

Now that you know about the different layers of a person's aura, it is time to learn some tips for viewing it. To see auras, understand the way energy feels in your body. You can do that by closing your eyes, aligning your breath, then asking the aura colors to appear in front of you. Your goal is to reach a state of relaxed awareness, so you can view auras without problems.

What's good about learning how to view and read auras is that it provides you with endless possibilities and opportunities. Furthermore, learning how to read and protect the aura that your own body portrays can improve not only your spiritual health, but also your emotional and physical health.

Fortunately, honing your aura viewing and reading ability does not require you to become a mystic. In fact, you can start developing this skill by following simple steps and tips, like the following:

Learn about the different colors of the aura

Note that auras exist in different colors, with each one conveying a message or information about the object or person that they surround. You need to study them and what each one means. The basic colors of aura that you have to be aware of if you want to be able to view and read them accurately are the following:

- **Red** – This color represents the heart, physical body, and circulation. You can view it as a positive light. This color is a sign of a healthy ego. In some cases, it can also indicate anxiety and anger as well as one's unforgiving nature.

- **Yellow** – Another color of aura is yellow, which can be connected to the life energy and spleen. This color manifests awakening, creativity, intelligence, inspiration, optimism, and playfulness. It also indicates the easy-going nature of a person. However, there are also instances when bright yellow signals the fear of losing power, control, respect, and prestige.

- **Orange** – Orange is also another popular color of aura. You can link it to one's emotions and reproductive organs. If you look at it positively then it can indicate stamina, energy, productivity, love for adventure, courage, and being social or outgoing. However, there are also negative connotations to this color, such as stress associated with addiction.

- **Blue** – This color pertains to the thyroid and throat. You can link this color to a person's loving and caring nature, as well as their sensitivity and intuition. Darker shades of this color, however, indicate negativity, such as the fear of telling or facing the truth, as well as of self-expression and the future.

- **Violet** – This is the color of aura, which can be connected to the nervous system, pineal gland, and the crown. Note that violet is the wisest and the most sensitive color out of the many aura colors. It is also an intuitive color, which can reveal one's psychic power associated with self-attunement.

- **Green** – This color can be linked to the lungs and heart. Once you see it in a person's aura, you can immediately sense balance and growth. It also usually results in change. It indicates a person's love for nature and the people and animals surrounding them. However, a muddy or dark shade of green shown in a person's aura indicates low self-esteem, insecurity, resentment, and jealousy.

- **Gold** – This color represents divine protection and enlightenment. Having a gold aura means that you can always ask for guidance from the highest good.

- **Black** – This color tends to pull or draw energy and transform it. In most cases, a black aura manifests your inability to forgive. It can also indicate an unreleased grief. There are some instances when this color of aura can result in health issues.

- **White** – This color represents truth and purity. It also means that there are angels close to you. In some cases, having this aura means that a woman is pregnant.

Familiarizing yourself with these colors is crucial in honing the skill of viewing and reading auras. The presence of colors in auras is the key to reading those around you accurately. To improve the way you see these colors, stay in a neutral-colored room and then play with objects that have brighter colors. Close your eyes then breathe deeply while asking the different colors to present themselves in front of you.

Look at the color while taking deep breaths. In this case, an object wrapped in a solid color is what you should be looking at. Let your gaze soften in such a way that you're looking right through it. After that, observe the field surrounding the colored object. This is where you will notice a pale color that comes out of it.

Once you improve your ability to read single colors, add multi-colored objects in a gradual manner. This is helpful in expanding your psychic vision and mastering the ability to read auras.

Begin by seeing energy

Some people have a natural ability to see auras, making them different from the average person. What makes these naturally gifted people different is their full awareness of all the energies surrounding them. With that in mind, it is safe to say that sensing energy is crucial in aura reading.

Start by sensing the energy within your body. After mastering that, you can begin attempting to sense the energy radiated by other people.

Use magic eye puzzles

If you are not yet familiar with magic eye puzzles, then note these are images that you can use to learn to view and read auras. They work in training your brain to find something that does not seem to appear at first glance. Remember that successfully detecting the hidden images inside a magic eye puzzle can train your brain to remember how you can uncover such messages again the future. It can also help you realize that in most cases, there are a lot of hidden messages from what your naked eyes can see at first glance.

Practice viewing at least one magic eye image every day. Doing this is helpful in shifting your awareness, making it possible for your brain to realize that by trying to relax your eyes, you can reveal something more than what meets your naked eye. This is beneficial if you want to start seeing auras. With the magic eye images, you can get rid of some filters from the mind, allowing you to go deeper into it.

Improve your ability to detect the picture inside the magic eye images. After mastering this ability, you can begin to practice shifting the picture in and out of your focus. Look around the image within the magic eye picture without losing it. Also, pay close attention to the manner through which you were able to stimulate the inner image to reveal itself. You can use such technique once you start mastering aura reading.

Practice viewing auras in the mirror

Sit or stand in front of a mirror then look at your reflection. Transfer your focus into a point, which goes beyond your body. For example, this could be on top of your right shoulder.

Look at this space and relax. Let the hidden information related to the aura appear. In the beginning, what you will see is just a white energy outline surrounding you, which is actually a good thing. Maintain your focus, then let the white energy expand and wait for it to be filled with color.

Use crystals and plants

Crystals and plants are also among the things that you can use in seeing and reading auras. You can use them especially if you experience problems viewing your own aura. Crystals and plants can also help during practice. What you have to do to take advantage of them is to let a crystal or plant sit in front of you. If possible, put it in a place with a white background. Look just beyond the crystal or plant's border. It should seem like you're viewing a magic eye image.

Relax and focus until the crystal or plant's energy field starts to appear. Once it appears, your next step is to figure out what the plant or crystal tells you based on its energy. For instance, you need to tell whether the energy emitted by the plant is healthy and happy, or not. If you're using a crystal, find out if the aura it emits is bright and clear; otherwise, you need to recharge and cleanse it.

Improve your mind's eye

In most cases, people who want to develop clairvoyance experience frustration during the process because they look at this psychic ability the wrong way. Clairvoyance is the psychic ability to gather information regarding a person, physical event, object, or location using your extrasensory perception. Viewing information clairvoyantly is not the same as viewing such information using your physical eyes.

It is possible for you to improve your ability to spot images using your mind's eye by letting your imagination work. You also need to tap into your ability to receive mental images. One exercise that will surely work in your favor is to imagine a tree. Does it have pine needles or leaves? Can you use your mind to tune into the tree's aura? Is there a field of light surrounding the tree each time you look at it?

Imagination is linked closely to the clairvoyant and psychic sight, which is why you have to develop it if you want to improve your clairvoyance, too. Another practice exercise that you can do is to think of a loved one. Get a mental image of the person you're thinking about and determine what his/her aura looks like.

Observe the mental picture of the appearing aura. Avoid judging it. Don't worry too much about your accuracy for now. What you should focus on is having fun while improving your mind's eye. Accuracy will follow through constant practice and persistence. Try this specific exercise on your own, too. Imagine yourself using your mind's eye to visualize your own aura, and observe what you see.

Improve your vibration

One of the key secrets to honing a spiritual gift or psychic skill is an improved vibration. Remember that fear and doubt have the tendency of hindering your ability to view and read auras. Aside from that, viewing auras will also be blocked by your limiting beliefs and thoughts. In this case, you have to lift up your vibration. The whole process involves getting rid of filters, limiting beliefs, and negativity from your life.

You also need to integrate love, light, joy, and positivity into your life. Having a loving and happy heart can directly align with your goal of opening up your psychic skills and spiritual gifts. Quieting your mind and connecting with your angels can help, too. Focus on meditating, laughing, and enjoying life. All these positive acts can help raise your vibration, which is also the key to aligning with your ability to view auras, listen to angels, and live your authentic truth.

Aside from these strategies, it pays to be persistent and to continue practicing. Note that constant practice is the key to developing your ability to see and read auras. Set a specific intention to begin viewing auras and perform the tips and exercises mentioned in this chapter. It also helps to raise your awareness in the "now".

Chapter 5 – The Third Eye

Third eye awakening should also be part of psychic development. The third eye, which is located between the eyes at the pineal gland, serves as the gateway to the divine realm. It is actually your sixth chakra and is key to unlocking your sixth sense. By opening up your third eye, you gain clear insight, a strong connection or relationship with your inner wisdom or intuition, an intellectual balance, and a high level of open-mindedness.

You can expect your higher wisdom and intuition to come even more alive if you allow this specific energy center to be well-balanced and fully open. While accessing your sixth sense is quite challenging, not to mention frightening, especially if you're not used to seeing things that other people can't see, it actually has plenty of benefits. Here are just some of the benefits of successfully opening up your third eye:

- **Improves your mental power** – In some cases, you lose your focus or concentration mainly because you have a blurry or imbalanced third eye. You need a clear mental ability if you want to formulate good decisions. Such mental clarity can help you find solutions to certain problems. Opening up your third eye can boost your mental power. It lets you find solutions and raise your self-awareness. In addition, third eye awakening makes it possible to deal with daily stress and your emotions better.

- **Allows you to stay away from negativity** – It is natural for humans to worry about things that are beyond their control. Aside from that, people also tend to hold on to negative emotions, even those that they felt long ago. If you awaken your third eye, you can free yourself from all these negative emotions. It allows you to be in the present, which is often full of beauty, not pain and sorrow from the past. Third eye awakening also raises your awareness of your surroundings. It lets you focus on the present, instead of the pain in your past.

- **Promotes the flow of great ideas** – There are instances when you will experience mental clutter, causing you to have a hard time figuring out what idea is the best or what path you should take. This scenario might block a new idea from coming in. By opening up your third eye, you can clear your mind and body from these blockages. Once you remove all these blocks, you can expect new and great ideas to flow freely. Third eye awakening also makes you more receptive and open to ideas that can make your life even more exciting and enjoyable.

- **Makes living your purpose less challenging** – This is because third eye awakening promotes ease and flow when it comes to living your specific purpose. Note that this process is challenging for many, considering the fact that trying to live one's purpose has plenty of twists and turns. With third eye awakening, you will be able to get in touch with your spirit guides who can guide you in case you get stuck. They can also offer guidance in case you wish to obtain extra clarity or have some form of friendly encouragement.

- **Promotes self-acceptance and self-love** – Another benefit of awakening your third eye is that it lets you connect with spirit guides that can provide you with unconditional love. Your spirit guides will also be around to support you during your times of need. This is usually enough to make some positive changes in how you deal with yourself. Your relationship with yourself and that of others will be even better as you learn self-love and self-acceptance.

- **Gets rid of confusion and indecision from all aspects of your life** – Third eye awakening can improve your ability to call upon your personal spirit guides. You can call them in times of need. They can guide you each time you face challenges. Your spirit guides can also help you gain new understandings and insights about your problems. They can even help to get rid of your confusions, doubts, and indecisions.

How to Awaken your Third Eye?

The benefits of third eye awakening are not just limited to the ones mentioned above. Note that your third eye serves as your head's intuition. It plays a vital part in your overall wellbeing. It represents a higher level of consciousness, making it possible for you to perceive the world. The problem is that if it gets constricted or blocked, you will also experience certain problems, like insomnia, lack of purpose, overthinking, narrow-mindedness, and suffocating beliefs.

A blocked or constricted third eye might also cause you to be unable to connect with your own soul. If you wish to build a strong relationship with your soul and connect to your inner purpose, then you must know some ways to awaken your third eye. With the help of certain techniques, you can awaken this chakra and use it to gain a more enlightened and deeper understanding of the universe surrounding you.

Nurture silence

You have to know exactly how to silence your mind as this plays a major role in awakening your third eye. It could be through meditation, getting in touch with nature, or letting yourself get absorbed into something you love, like a sports practice, or your favorite art.

You need to nurture silence, since third eye perception can elevate your senses to a subtle level. For you to listen intently to the information and messages sent to you by your third eye, it is crucial to listen to its whispers. Silence your mind and prevent it from getting messed up. Note that allowing your mind to get too noisy or busy might result in your inability to grasp the main message.

Improve your creativity

You need to hone your creativity, too, if you want to awaken your third eye. You have to allow your creativity to flow freely all the time. You can do that by engaging in activities that require you to be creative. One example is to try learning a new craft or art. Avoid being a perfectionist, though. Just look for inspiration and let your imagination and creativity come loose without putting too much pressure on yourself.

Improving your creativity is a vital part of third eye awakening as it is one way of loosening your rational mind. This means that you will no longer have to deal with your somewhat uncontrollable mental chatter, which constantly comments on each step you take and whether you are right or wrong. You no longer have to worry about it controlling all your actions with an intended outcome or a certain agenda.

You need to calm your mind, especially the part which tends to control your reality and influence your creativity. By having a calmer mind, you can open up more space to let the capacity of your third eye blossom and unfold.

Meditate

Meditation is an effective technique for third eye awakening. It raises your awareness of your own thoughts, giving you the chance to access the mental clarity linked to your third eye much better. You need to meditate to let your mind rest on one object or thought. Just make sure that you pick the right environment and surroundings to meditate. It should be a place where you feel completely comfortable and at peace.

Some people tend to feel more open-minded and peaceful if they meditate close to nature. If you are one of them, then meditating outdoors is perfect for you. Look for a space with a comfortable temperature. It should also be a spot where you can sit peacefully without distractions.

You can also try indoor meditation. What you have to do is to designate a space in your home where you can meditate. Generally, you will need a cushion, which you can use to sit on the floor more comfortably. Soothing music and some candles are also necessary. When you meditate, remember that it is a personal process. This means that you have to pick the most suitable environment for you.

Use crystals and precious stones

Crystals serve as your influential allies during the third eye awakening process. With that in mind, it is advisable to start using gemstones and crystals that have the violet, indigo, and purple color palettes. Such colors can awaken, nurture, align, balance, and cultivate your third eye. You should bring your chosen precious stones and crystals with you anytime you wish to unlock or awaken your sixth sense.

One of the stones that you can use to awaken your third eye is the purple fluorite, which is a semi-precious gem designed to sharpen your intuition and free your mind of muddled thoughts. Another choice is amethyst, which is a precious stone traditionally used to relieve third eye headaches and perform other forms of healing. It also represents wisdom. You can also use black obsidian, which is a famous member of the group composed of third eye crystals. It promotes the right balance between reason and emotion.

Take processed foods out of your diet

Cutting out processed foods completely is crucial in awakening your third eye. Note that the human body is not built in such a way that it can digest large amounts of processed carbs, sugar, and fats that are often present in fast and convenience foods. Your third eye can also benefit if you reduce your intake of animal meats. It is mainly because these meats have hormones that are not good for the development of your third eye.

As a replacement for processed foods, eat plenty of whole foods, like whole grains, nuts, and legumes, as well as fruits and veggies. Aside from making you feel full, these foods are good and healthy for your body. They are also easy to digest. You have to improve your daily diet and remove those foods that are bad for you, as proper diet has a direct influence on your hormones and energy levels. With that in mind, it is safe to say that they can influence your thoughts and feelings.

Drink herbs that promote third eye cleansing

What is good about cleansing herbs is that they work effectively in recalibrating your third eye. Start drinking herbal teas to gain those benefits associated with psychic development. Among the best herbal teas, in this case, are those that have Gingko Biloba, Gotu Kola, passionflower, and rosemary.

Practice grounding

Awakening your third eye abilities often requires you to let your feet land on the ground first. Grounding can help you gain energy and allow it to run through your entire body and energy system. Such can create a healthy opening for the subtle channels of perception to come out. Activating your third eye might cause you to gather information that appears a bit unfamiliar, disturbing, or unusual to those who don't have the skill.

Also, being grounded and gaining enough energy is a major help in expanding your perception's subtle judgments. It helps you stay away from the most common negative signs of opening up the third eye, like confusion and the feeling of being disoriented. It also lets you open up your third eye in a gradual manner, thereby allowing you to cultivate a reliable foundation first before moving into boosting your discernment and ability to interpret extrasensory perceptions.

Develop your intuition

Your third eye actually serves as the center of your higher wisdom, vision, and insight, so it is definitely a big help in developing your intuition if you want to open it up. Fortunately, there are several ways to hone your intuition. You can try acquainting yourself with your dreams as well as their meanings. You can also try lucid dreaming or learn the basics of reading tarot cards or a horoscope. Just look for ways to cultivate your intuition and apply them to your daily activities.

The main reason why you need to hone such a skill when awakening your sixth sense is that your third eye is the core of higher levels of intuition and perception. You can learn about other ways to develop your intuition and obtain more confidence in this specific psychic ability in the next chapter of this book.

Once you have practiced the strategies listed above, assess yourself from time to time to figure out if you have made some progress. You will instantly know that you are successful in awakening your third eye if you display the following signs:

- A feeling of pressure in between your two eyebrows

- Ability to sense warning signs or alerts for next actions

- A higher intuition

- A higher sensitivity to light

- Increased pressure on the head, possibly leading to headaches

- A higher sensitivity to anything that is toxic

- Healthy and conscious eating

- A new perception of everything

- A higher connectivity with almost everything

- Changes in your thought patterns

- Constantly experiences vivid and lucid dreaming

- Increased synchronicities

Third eye awakening serves as your doorway to all things related to psychic development, including astral projection, telepathy, lucid dreaming, and clairvoyance. By cultivating your connection to your third eye, you can clearly separate yourself from spirits. You can also start connecting the metaphysical methods of being to your third eye, including how you can go beyond human's limitations, how you can walk between realities, and how to wake up from a dream.

However, you have to remember that there are also dangers to awakening your third eye. The fact that it is a sensitive part of your body makes it possible for you to see the unseen. There is also a great chance for you to fall into delusion. Fortunately, training yourself by raising your awareness can balance the things that you see with your third eye.

By raising your awareness, you can prevent yourself from getting hurt due to this gift. You can also avoid controlling people or telling them something they would not want to hear with this psychic ability. In addition, you can stay away from negative experiences that might result from awakening your third eye by working with a spiritual guide. Just make sure that you ground yourself and look for a teacher who can help you gain a full understanding of your experience.

Also, avoid rushing into the experience. It would be best to take things slow and allow yourself to go with the natural flow of opening up your third eye. With that, you can develop a vibrant and open third eye, which aids in letting the highest level of ethereal energy enter your body. You can also develop some abilities after awakening your third eye, including insight, intuition, concentration, decisiveness, bliss, and clarity.

Chapter 6 – How to Strengthen your Intuition

Having a strong intuition allows you to enjoy far more than just getting psychic messages. Intuition refers to the immediate awareness, knowledge, and understanding taken from neither reasoning nor perception. In fact, it is an effortless and automatic feeling, which frequently motivates you to take action quickly. Your intuition tends to speak to you all the time. It is the small voice, gut feeling, hunch, or last-minute decision that comes to your mind.

However, you need to listen to it and choose to act on it to receive proper intuitive guidance. If you want to hone your intuition and enjoy its benefits, then it would be ideal to learn about its different types first. In this chapter we will list the different ways that intuition can manifest itself.

Clairvoyance

Also called clear seeing, clairvoyance is the most popular yet the least understood gift of intuition. Having this ability can be likened to watching a movie within your head. It lets you see things within your mind in the form of pictures, impressions, symbols, or short movies. Many consider it as the most symbolic out of the different types of intuitive abilities.

Clairvoyance often makes use of a chakra found in your forehead as a means of developing your intuition. This chakra is known as the third eye, which was already discussed in the previous chapter. Your third eye chakra, once awakened, will perceive subtle energy wavelengths and patterns then translate these details through your developing clairvoyance into clear impressions or images.

The images will most likely appear on a screen in your mind. They may come in the form of symbols, colors, or movies. There are also instances when they may become holographic in nature.

Generally, the pictures serve as your own movie projector. They may also come in the form of quick impressions that tend to create a certain visual using your mind's eye.

People whose clairvoyant ability are predominant also tend to have vivid dreams triggered by awakening their intuition. If you wish to develop clairvoyance, then make it a point to look for pictures that tend to pop into your mind all of a sudden. These images might be intuitive messages sent to you. Be patient while developing your ability to see these images. Eventually, you will notice your clairvoyance growing.

Clairsentience

Also known as clear feeling, clairsentience is another intuitive ability that an aspiring psychic should hone. This ability makes it possible for you to sense or feel important information in your body. In most cases, you will receive such information in the form of feelings that go through your third chakra. If you have this ability, then you will most likely have gut reactions to certain situations or events.

You can feel the information in any part of your body, which is also referred to as a body clue. For instance, if you talk to someone with a fever, then you may start feeling feverish, too, because of your awakened intuition. Clairsentience is actually known as the most sensitive out of all the different intuitive abilities. This is because it lets you feel the emotions of other people.

However, take note that even though this ability represents the most genuinely compassionate and empathic out of all intuitive skills, it still tends to create some confusion for many. This is because having this skill makes it possible for you to pick up all the details surrounding you. This frequently leads to confusion since you will most likely lose touch with your own emotional and physical feelings, and instead will be triggered by feeling the emotions of others.

If you do not work on honing this skill properly, then you will most likely be drowned by all the noise brought on by your awakened intuition and get overwhelmed in the process. To handle all the feelings you receive, it would be helpful to write them down in a journal. This will give you an idea about the number of clairsentient messages you receive using your intuition. By recognizing the messages, you can pick up more of them each day without confusing them with your own feelings.

Clairaudience

Clairaudience is an intuitive ability, which lets you hear important details inside your mind. This ability is also called clear hearing. You may receive the details as sounds, lyrics, songs, or statements. You may also sense them in the form of vibrations. Many consider it as the easiest out of the different intuitive and psychic abilities, because you can listen to it.

Those who have this skill tend to receive intuitive details through a part of the body situated above their ears and below their temples. Such part of the human brain tends to cover the temporal lobe, the specific place where you process auditory information. If you develop this ability, then you will most likely feel comfortable with your own voice. This increases the possibility of honing your intuition just by differentiating your ego voice and intuitive voice.

By doing that, you can figure out the major differences in the tone once you hear various information. Your intuitive voice or your inner calm is actually subtle, loving, and calm. Such awakening intuition gives you empowerment and confidence. On the other hand, your ego voice tends to be authoritative, demanding, demeaning, and critical. It is a bit harsh and might cause you to feel powerless.

This is the main reason why you need to meditate regularly if you want to develop clairaudience and maximize its benefits. Through regular meditation, you can discern between your developing intuitive voice and your ego voice. If you successfully develop this skill, then you get the chance to read the energy of others by listening to the messages sent to you.

Claircognizance

Also called clear knowing, this is the last intuitive ability that aspiring psychics should develop. Having this type of intuition gives you the ability to perceive or see information in the form of a hunch or impression. Many consider this to be the strongest intuitive ability as it lets you receive information instantly. It will also give you an idea about what works and what does not.

You can receive the information provided by this intuitive ability through at least one part of your body. It could be the crown or the heart chakra. In most cases, the intuitive information can be likened to a warm feeling emanating from your chest. You may also feel it rushing through the topmost part of your head. You can receive it as a complete statement or idea.

Someone known for being a great judge of character can be considered as claircognizant. Those with visions about the future or prophetic dreams through their developing intuition also display claircognizance.

How to Develop and Strengthen your Intuition?

Regardless of the type of intuitive ability you wish to develop, you will feel pleased to know that you can hone it with a few exercises and strategies that you can practice regularly. Here are some of them:

Write in a journal.

Journaling can encourage a stream of consciousness that is helpful in honing your intuition. Also, take note that intuitive messages tend to be subtle. They are at risk of fading from your conscious mind quickly. This is the main reason why you have to take action by recording them. Remember that if you do not capture your intuitive insights, you may not be able to recall them after just a few seconds.

Through journaling, accessing your intuition and capturing the wisdom behind it will be easier. Fortunately, you only need 5 to

10 minutes every day to do it. This short amount of time will bring amazing clarity to whatever comes to your mind.

Meditate.

You need to meditate on a regular basis if you want to cultivate your intuition because it is effective in clearing your mind. It helps get rid of unnecessary thoughts and worries. It also prevents you from overthinking. One great thing about meditation is that it does not take too long. In fact, five to ten minutes of meditation daily is enough to help you stay attuned to your deeper desires, needs, and feelings.

Each time you meditate, you will notice some insights coming up. These insights might also come up after you meditate, especially when your state of mind is calmer and more centered. Make sure that you pay close attention to all the ideas and insights that come to your mind during and after meditation, as these help to develop your intuition.

Work with your altered states and dreams.

Dreams are important in honing your intuition because they serve as a way for your subconscious mind to process information and deal with unacknowledged longings, repressed feelings, and internal stress. In most cases, your dreams are symbolic and provide deep messages. It would be best to familiarize yourself with the most common dream symbols. Such will let you understand what your dreams mean and what your intuition tells you through them.

Working with your dreams is possible with a simple exercise. The first thing that you have to do is to get a paper and pen then put it beside you before you sleep at night. Once you lay down, request for a dream from your intuition mentally. Repeat your request several times before you finally fall asleep.

Upon waking up in the morning, get the paper and pen and write down or draw anything that comes to your mind. Do this even if there is nothing specific that you remember. Evaluate what you have put down on paper as this will give you an idea about the messages that you have received. Act on it where appropriate.

Test your gut feelings or hunches.

If you often have hunches, then it is helpful to test them to figure out if they will come true. For instance, if you sensed that it would rain the next day, then consider writing this down so you can check if your hunch is right. Write down anything that you feel or think will happen anytime soon.

By writing these things down, you can easily check whether your guess was right later on. Doing this will let you know whether you indeed have the gift of intuition, and if your ability is improving or not.

Set aside a space for reflection.

You can't expect your intuition to flourish in a noisy and busy environment. Whether you are at work or at home, it is necessary to have a spot where you can reflect peacefully. It is necessary for clearly hearing your insights from deep inside. You can do that by reflecting on your experiences in a peaceful environment.

You should also make it a point to set aside some time for reflection every day. Some tools for reflection that you can use are journaling, walking to clear your head of unwanted and messy thoughts, and cultivating a mindfulness or meditation practice. A simple exercise that you can do is to spend some time each day building your awareness of how you exactly feel. Scan your body and check and reflect on your feelings regularly. By doing that, it is possible for you to be in touch with what your instinct or gut is telling you.

Observe your body compass.

Note that your intuition tends to talk to you using your body. By cultivating more awareness of your own body, you can raise your sensitivity to your own intuition. If you feel uncomfortable when you are on the verge of making a decision, then pay close attention to what you feel.

Are your feelings light or heavy? Do you feel sick in your gut? Whatever you feel may be a result of a stress response that a false fear has activated. However, this may also be your intuition sending you a loud and clear message, so you really need to observe your feelings and body closely.

Practice creative visualization.

You can also use the creative visualization technique when planning to tap into your intuition. This technique involves closing your eyes and using your imagination as a means of creating your life's desires. It opens up new creative energies designed to let you tap your intuition.

One way to do creative visualization is to spend several minutes breathing through your diaphragm. Remove any thoughts from your mind and visualize them fading away. Imagine that you are lying inside a cave without any clothes on. Feel the moisture coming from the ceiling while its acidic nature starts dissolving your bodily systems, organs, and skin. You should also imagine that you are a skeleton while still being fully aware.

Stripping yourself of everything can create a magical opening to your intuitive self. It is helpful in tapping your inner voice. While you can seek the help of a therapist to perform creative visualization, take note that it is possible to do it on your own.

Chapter 7 – Spirit Guides and How You can Connect with Them

Your spirit guides also play a vital role in psychic development. Spirit guides refer to incorporeal beings assigned to you before you are born. They are the ones who will guide you through life. One of the responsibilities of your spirit guide is to help you in fulfilling the spiritual contract you made with yourself before your incarnation.

Everyone has a spirit team composed of angels and spirit guides who are sent to guide, teach, and protect them at various stages of their life. Some of these guides will stay with you your whole life. Others, on the other hand, will just pop in occasionally so you will be guided in certain parts of your life and in fulfilling your goals. Your spirit guides help you by tuning in to your energy first, and then directing you to help you accomplish your earthly mission.

They look out for you, guide you and encourage you to fulfill your soul's objectives as well as your life intentions. They work as your guardian angels and life guides whom you can expect to stay with you 100 percent of the time – from the time you were born up to your death. You can also connect to spirit guides who tend to come and go based on your specific areas of focus, and present lessons and questions.

Here is a brief overview of the most common spirit guides whom you can connect with, and can assist you in making the most out of your life:

Guardian Spirit Guides

Your guardian spirit guides serve as your protectors. They are capable of interfering with your life physically with the aim of protecting you. With that in mind, they are the ones who can prevent you from getting harmed and can create an energetic field to surround and protect you from any form of danger. It is possible for you to connect to your guardian spirit guide anytime you feel the need for protection.

Messenger Spirit Guides

You can expect these spirit guides to appear in your life when you are preparing to walk a new path or enter a new chapter of your life. They are the ones who will prepare you in a new endeavor by providing you with important information you may need. They deliver their messages through symbols and signs, so you can formulate sound decisions.

Your messenger guides will also most likely appear when you are preparing to make a huge life decision, or each time you are at a crossroad. Their goal is to support you in your decision while providing you with insights on the ideal course of action. Among the things they use to communicate with you are number patterns, dreams, symbols, and synchronicities.

For you to get the help of your messenger guides, you just need to ask them to be part of your life. Continue having an open dialogue with your spirit guides regarding your concerns and questions. They will offer you answers, provided you are willing and open to listen to their messages.

Gatekeeper Spirit Guides

The main goal of your gatekeeper spirit guides is to provide you with access to the various portals of the spiritual world. Serving as gatekeepers between several dimensions, they can guide you in navigating the spiritual world safely. Working with your gatekeeper spirit guides can cultivate your intuition. They can also help in tapping into your psychic abilities and letting you experience situations related to honing your psychic skills, like astral projection and lucid dreaming.

With your gatekeeper spirit guides around, you can gain protection each time you decide to travel deeply into the spiritual world, especially if you are unprepared. They can keep you safe from bad spirits and negative entities. In addition, they are the ones who can facilitate a positive journey after your death.

Healing Spirit Guides

These spirit guides, as their name suggests, are capable of healing your energetic, physical, and emotional stresses and ailments. You will receive spiritual and emotional support each time you need it when you are with your healing spirit guides. They are present when you are undergoing a surgery or dealing with a pain or illness. You can call them if you want to speed up your healing process, or each time you feel down or undergo emotional trauma.

Healing guides often work together with the people in the healing industry. They frequently serve as facilitators and mentors to those who are trying to heal others. As such, it is usually possible to feel the presence of your healing spirit guide if you are part of the healing profession.

Other types of spirit guides who tend to hover around people are past life friends, deceased loved ones, angels, spirit animals, deities, and ascended masters. If you want to be able to connect to your spirit guides and ask them to guide you in various stages and aspects of your life, then make it a point to apply these tips and practices regularly:

Have faith in them

Remember that your spirit guides won't be able to communicate with you if you do not believe in them. So, start tuning in to them and have faith about their existence. One way to start believing in their presence is to think about specific moments when you felt like you were saved, helped, or redirected with the aid of some unknown and unfamiliar force.

Note that spirit guides tend to come into your life using various means. With that, spend time each day to listen to your mind, spirit, and body. Allow yourself to be in the moment of complete stillness. While you are in that state, you might be able to receive clear messages that often appear in the form of pictures in your head, a voice or sound, or a feeling or smell. Make it a point to write down anything that you hear, feel, see, and smell as these might be intuitive messages sent to you by your spirit guides.

Use crystals to meditate

Some crystals, such as amethyst, contain powerful intuitive properties, which is the reason why you can use them to meditate while aiming to connect to your spirit guides. Amethyst is a brilliant and purple crystal linked to your third eye chakra, which is associated with your higher self and intuition.

Meditating with an amethyst and putting it directly on your brow can heighten your spiritual awareness since it can elevate you into a higher level of consciousness. This can further strengthen your intuition, which serves as a direct gateway to your spirit guide.

Listen to what your intuition tells you

The little voice you hear that tells you something, such as to slow down or be more cautious, is actually a message from your higher self or spirit guide who communicates with you directly. Try to listen to what your intuition tells you and see its results. If listening to your intuition often produces good results, then it is probably a message sent to you by your spirit guide.

Make it a habit to ask for their guidance

Your spirit guides are capable of guiding you with anything. You can seek their help for tasks as simple as finding a car park, to more complicated stuff, like mending your broken heart, finding enough courage to chase after your dream, or finding the most fulfilling job.

When it comes to connecting to your spirit guides, take note that there is no request that is too small, too big, too broad, or too specific. Just make it a habit to ask for their guidance so they can step in and connect to you.

Build your sacred space

You need a sacred space where you can connect with and communicate with your spirit guides on a daily basis. Your sacred space could be a bedside table, one corner of your room, or a window ledge. Spend some time there every day so you can connect with your guides. You need to invest some time with your guides, so you can make your relationship with them grow.

Practice intuitive writing

Intuitive writing is actually one of the most effective ways to communicate and connect with higher realms. What you have to do to practice this technique is to clear your sacred space first. Do that by lighting a candle and sit calmly and peacefully with a couple of colored pens and a journal.

Use the first colored pen to write a question in your journal. You should then take the second pen and ask your spirit guides to give an answer to your question. Allow the response of your spirit guides to flow naturally from your hand down to the journal.

Have a spirit guide diary

This is where you should write any vision, intuitive hunch, dream, or guidance you receive. Keep in mind that if you want to connect with your guides, then you need to take note of and believe in the intuitive help and guidance they offer as soon as you receive it. By writing it down, you will have a record of what you received from them, including their messages.

Learn about the ways through which your spirit guides try to contact you

Your spirit guides may be trying to communicate with you in different ways, so you have to be aware of methods they often use to contact humans. This could be in the form of a meaningful coincidence. Each time your spirit guides try to help you, strange coincidences may occur in your life. This might indicate that a spirit guide is trying to draw your attention. Take note of any coincidences that happen in your life right now. Doing that can help you recognize the guidance offered to you by your spirit guides.

Spirit guides may also contact you through significant objects. They often offer guidance by putting objects in front of you. These objects play a major role in your journey. It could be in the form of coins on your path, or white feathers from the sky that landed at your feet. Some of the significant objects sent to you by your spirit guides are actually their little gifts. You can use them as a motivation to continue on your journey.

Your spirit guides may also appear in your visions or dreams to give you the guidance you need. For instance, if you are asleep or meditating, the busiest portion of your mind will become still and quiet. This will allow you to hear the voices of your spirit guides.

With that in mind, it is best to have a dream diary near you. This is where you should write down your dreams, so you can analyze them later. Avoid using a dream dictionary when trying to analyze your dreams, though. What you have to do, instead, is to think about and reflect on the meaning of the events in your dream. You should also analyze their relationship with your present life circumstances.

If you strongly feel that your spirit guide is trying to communicate with you, then you have to silence your rational mind and tune into your intuition. You can achieve this by spending quality time with nature, and in prayer or meditation. Connecting to your spirit guide also requires you to be more open-minded. This will open up more opportunities for your spirit guide to give you the support and encouragement you need to continue your life journey.

Chapter 8 – Mistakes to Avoid When Developing your Psychic Abilities

Now that you know some of the most common psychic abilities, the benefits of developing them, and how you can actually cultivate and develop them, it is time to understand the mistakes and blockages to psychic development that you have to avoid. You have to be aware of these mistakes, so you will not end up making errors when you are trying to hone your psychic powers.

Lacking in belief

Do you believe that the psychic phenomena and psychic abilities are real? Most likely you will answer yes to that question. However, take note that the real question here is what your subconscious mind believes in. Remember that if your subconscious mind does not believe in your psychic abilities, such as your ability to see auras, then regardless of how hard you try, you will never be able to see auras or turn yourself into a real psychic.

You need to reprogram your mind, so it will start to have faith in your psychic abilities. You can do that through intense practice and affirmations. It is important to reprogram your beliefs through affirmations and cleanse your negative experiences through emotional healing. That way, your subconscious mind will no longer lose faith in your ability.

Ingesting toxic substances

If you want to develop your psychic ability, then you also need to stay away from toxic substances, like drugs, alcohol, and cigarettes. These are unhealthy and toxic substances that might cause you to develop an overindulgent and unhealthy habit. Such behavior can affect your progress while honing your psychic skills. Any type of abuse in the use of toxic substances can cause your negative emotional attachments to get attached to your auric field. This might cause you to leak out your energy and lower your vibration.

Not having a protected and safe working environment

You need to create a well-protected and safe spot for your spiritual practices, like healings, readings, and meditation. Your chosen spot should also be kept energetically clean to prevent any unwanted energy from coming in.

Not knowing your limitations

As an aspiring psychic, you need to set boundaries and be aware of your own limitations. Note that your lack of awareness of your limitations is dangerous to your ability. Using your psychic ability when you are too tired, sick, or in a place that is emotionally unhealthy can increase your risk of losing your power. You have to be honest with yourself and the boundaries and limitations you have set.

Harboring hate and aggression

Keep in mind that your psychic mind does not have any room for hate or aggression. Filling your mind and heart with hate and aggression will cause difficulties in psychic development. You need to remove all negative emotions to be a more effective psychic.

You might also be shutting the door towards developing your psychic abilities if you fear the responsibilities that come with the gift. Still, it is advisable to keep your door open, especially if you really have the gift. Also, keep in mind that the psychic development process is not that complicated.

You simply need to start with energy work and doing some simple practices designed to improve a particular psychic ability. In addition, you need to identify the blockages, such as the ones mentioned in this chapter that might ruin your chances of developing your psychic ability. Remove these blockages so you can continue seeing progress in your journey towards developing your psychic power.

Conclusion

Thanks again for taking the time to read this book!

You should now have a good understanding of psychic development!

If you enjoyed this book, please take the time to leave me a review on Amazon. I appreciate your honest feedback, and it really helps me to continue producing high quality books.